ML Answers the 101 Most-Asked Questions

The Catholic Wedding Answer Book

Also available in the ML ANSWERS THE 101 MOST-ASKED QUESTIONS series:

ML Answers the 101 Most-Asked Questions About Liturgy
   by Nick Wagner
The Lent, Triduum, and Easter Answer Book by Paul J. Niemann
The Liturgical Music Answer Book by Peggy Lovrien
The Catechumenate Answer Book by Paul Turner

ML Answers the 101 Most-Asked Questions

The Catholic Wedding Answer Book

Paul Turner

Resource Publications, Inc.
San Jose, California

Reprint Department
Resource Publications, Inc.
160 E. Virginia Street #290
San Jose, CA 95112-5876
(408) 286-8505 voice
(408) 287-8748 fax

Library of Congress Cataloging-in-Publication Data
Turner, Paul, 1953–
   The Catholic wedding answer book / Paul Turner.
     p. cm. — (ML answers the 101 most-asked questions)
   Includes bibliographical references and index.
   ISBN 0–89390–517–8
   1. Marriage—Religious aspects—Catholic Church—Miscellanea.
2. Catholic Church—Doctrines—Miscellanea. I. Title. II. Series.
BX2250 .T87 2001
264'.02085—dc21
                                    2001031875

01 02 03 04 05 | 5 4 3 2 1

Editorial director: Nick Wagner
Production: Romina Saha
Copyeditor: Tricia Joerger
Cover design: Nelson Estarija, Mike Sagara

OBLATA OCCASIONE FAVSTA
ANNIVERSARII XXV DIEI
INITARVM FELICITER NVPTIARVM
INTERROGATIONES ILLÆ
MICHAELI ET CYNTHIÆ TVRNER
DEDICANTVR INSCRIBVNTVR
QVORVM EXEMPLVM AMORIS
VNICA EST RESPONSIO
EADEM QVAM POSCVNT QVÆSITA

Contents

Preparing the Ceremony

The Ceremony

Acknowledgments

I wish to thank
The readers who wrote
Randy Calvo, Brian Torrey, and Jerry and Sally Cook, who read
The engaged, who hope
God, who loves.

P.T.

Introduction

You're engaged—congratulations! If you're planning a Catholic wedding, you probably have a lot of questions. I've got some answers for you.

Groundwork
Questions

1. May I be married outdoors or does a Catholic wedding have to be in a Catholic church?

Y ou probably may not have the wedding outdoors, but it depends. The answer comes from the *Code of Canon Law*, which contains the norms for the Roman Catholic Church. Canon 1118 considers two scenarios. First, if a Catholic marries another baptized person, the marriage should take place in the Catholic's parish church, but the local bishop can permit the marriage "in some other suitable place." Second, if the Catholic is marrying an unbaptized person the wedding happens in the Catholic's parish church "or in some other suitable place." In this second case, the bishop is not explicitly mentioned in the determination of the suitable place.

Defining the suitable place is a judgment call. Most commonly, authorities judge another suitable place to mean another church. In many dioceses, the bishop has ruled that outdoors is not suitable for any weddings, so even when one partner is unbaptized the pastor may not be able to permit an outdoor wedding. Ask your local Catholic parish to find out the rules for your area.

For Catholics, the church building is a sacred space symbolizing the people who worship there. We celebrate the most sacred events there—our sacraments, rituals in which we believe we encounter Christ most intimately. Because marriage is one of our sacraments, it deserves a sacred space. When you celebrate your wedding inside a church, you do so in a space where God most frequently and powerfully interacts with the community of believers.

> **2.** *May we have our wedding in a chapel or a home? I thought Mass could be celebrated anywhere.*

Weddings are usually restricted to churches (*Code of Canon Law* 1118). Parish churches are centers for the community of believers. They nurture the faith of those who seek marriage and provide a future home for their families. Although there are circumstances where the Eucharist (the Mass) is celebrated in other settings, we generally celebrate other sacraments like baptism and marriage in the parish church.

Dioceses may enact their own legislation in this regard. Some of them permit weddings in certain chapels, but others do not permit them there at all. Ask for the local rules at your Catholic parish.

3. *If the bishop doesn't allow weddings outside the church building and the priest does it anyway, will it still count?*

It will count if the priest has obtained the necessary authorization from the bishop. Catholic marriage has to observe the law of the church as well as that of the state. A priest witnesses marriage only at the approval of the bishop. (To be precise, a priest does not "marry you" nor "perform the ceremony"—he "witnesses" your marriage. More on this later.) If he acts without that approval, the church cannot verify that the wedding is valid—that it counts.

When you marry in the Catholic Church, your marriage takes on a spiritual dimension that enjoys the support of a community of believers. This limits some of your choices, such as place, but it gives you the church's assurance that the God we worship together will be an intimate part of your union.

4. We're living together. May we still be married in the Catholic Church?

It depends. The issue, of course, is sex. The Catholic Church does not approve of sex outside of marriage. We believe that sexual intercourse is a physical and spiritual expression of love that finds its purpose within a committed relationship. When sex takes place outside of marriage, it fails to accomplish the rare kind of love God meant it to signify. There are couples who live together but don't have sex and couples who have sex but don't live together. Most people assume that sex is part of cohabitation.

In any case, there is no universal Catholic law prohibiting a wedding for couples cohabiting before marriage nor for any couples having premarital sex. You could argue that living together does not interfere with your right to marriage (*Code of Canon Law* 1058). A typical pastor is generally disappointed with engaged couples who cohabit, but he usually works with them to arrange the wedding.

Nonetheless, there are pastors who think otherwise. Their responsibilities include preparing couples for the "holiness and duties of their new state" (c. 1063/2). If the pastor judges that living together does not constitute the proper preparation for the sacred state of marriage, he may say so. You might have options of lodging separately for a while, toning down the extravagance of the wedding, appealing to the bishop, or putting the wedding on hold.

Some pastors will want to give you extra attention because couples who cohabit before marriage have a higher incidence of infidelity and divorce than couples who don't. If you tell your pastor you made the decision to save money, he may challenge the attitude that thriftiness overcomes all other moral responsibility. The *Catechism of the Catholic Church* says sexual intercourse between unmarried persons "is gravely contrary to the dignity of persons and of human sexuality which is naturally ordered to the good of spouses and the generation and education of children" (2353).

If you're living together in a sexual relationship that differs from the ideals held by the Catholic Church, you should expect some questions about how you reconcile your desire for a Catholic marriage with your living arrangements.

5. I'm pregnant. May I have a Catholic wedding?

Probably. There is no law prohibiting the Catholic marriage of someone expecting a child.

However, concerns may come up similar to those with couples who live together before marriage. Are you aware of the Catholic Church's position on sex outside of marriage? How do you judge your own actions? When is it right and wrong for a couple to have sex? How do you reconcile your behavior with what the church teaches? How will you instruct your children about the rights and wrongs of sex outside of marriage?

You may also experience some difficulty arranging the wedding as quickly as you would like. Many couples in your situation want the wedding before the bride begins to show. But parishes usually want several months to work with couples to prepare them for marriage.

You have the option of waiting until after the child is born before the wedding takes place. This makes sense if you had not decided on marriage prior to the pregnancy. It will give you more time to think through your preparations and decision to marry. In fact, if there is any danger that your decision to marry is being forced by your pregnancy, it could jeopardize your freedom to marry and cause doubt about the validity of your union.

You are in an emotionally charged situation. You should be able to count on your parish church to help.

And please, carry the child to term. New life is always a gift from God. The life of your child is your highest priority.

6. My fiancé was married before. May we be married in the Catholic Church?

Yes, you may, but only if the previous marriage has been declared null or invalid by the Catholic Church, or if the former spouse is deceased. The church prohibits the marriage of anyone still bound by a prior union (*Code of Canon Law* 1085). If both those parties are still alive, a divorce decree is not enough. It settled matters for the state, but the church also needs assurance that no one asking for a marriage is already in one. All prior unions, except those in which the former spouse has died, need a declaration of nullity from the Catholic Church before either ex can have a Catholic wedding.

Annulments generally get started through the parish. Ask a parish minister to help you through the process. It usually involves gathering documentation about the previous marriage(s), obtaining written testimonies of the people involved and some folks who knew them, and waiting a while for church authorities to review all these records.

To many people, the thought of obtaining an annulment ranks up there with root canals, but the process can help people reflect on their past and bring some healing to the hurts.

7. Wait a minute. Even if my divorced fiancé is not a Catholic, married someone who was not a Catholic, and had the wedding completely apart from the Catholic Church — this person still needs an annulment in the Catholic Church?

Yes. The Catholic Church recognizes other marriages as binding, unless proven otherwise. Obviously, we proudly honor the good marriages of people in other religions. We assume all those marriages are forever, unless we can establish their nullity.

8. Then what does an annulment do?

An annulment establishes a divorced person's freedom to marry in the Catholic Church. Catholics believe that marriage is forever. If a marriage does not last, then it may not have been "marriage" as we understand marriage to be: a permanent union of love, freely chosen by responsible spouses, open to the gift of children. The annulment process asks whether the previous marriage fully qualified. One reason for wondering, obviously, is that the marriage did not last forever. If the annulment is granted, the church declares that the previous marriage should not be considered binding, and that frees the person for a Catholic wedding.

9. *I am a divorced Catholic, now engaged. My first marriage was not in a church. Do I need an annulment to marry in the Catholic Church?*

Yes, but it will probably be a simple matter. Catholics are expected to marry according to the Catholic form of marriage, which assumes marriage in a parish church. We do not bind people from other religions to the same rule. But if a Catholic marries without the proper form, we do not recognize the validity of the marriage. If the persons in that marriage divorce, an annulment can be granted on the grounds of "lack of form." Gather the documents such as the marriage license and the divorce decree to make your case, then contact your parish for help with this.

Even though the process is simpler than going through a full formal annulment case with written testimony from several people, remember the spiritual dimension of what is going on. God has been guiding you through several different chapters of your life to bring you to this new engagement. Be sure to reflect on your spiritual journey. Who has God been for you? How have you grown since your first marriage? Why do you want the church involved now when you didn't for the first marriage? How will your spiritual life be different with a wedding celebrated in church?

> **10.** If we don't want to have an annulment because it's too much work or too much money, or we don't agree with what an annulment means, may we just get the marriage blessed in a Catholic Church in a ceremony without Mass?

Whoa! First, please reconsider the annulment possibility. It can bring a lot of benefits to your spiritual life. You can experience a new peace with God and the church. If the cost is prohibitive, be sure to talk to someone at your parish about this. No one should be denied an annulment because of its expense.

Some people refuse to pursue annulments because they believe annulments mean "there was never a marriage" or that the children would be considered illegitimate. Remember, an annulment pertains to the spiritual nature of marriage. It does not deny that there was a wedding and family life; it affirms that the marriage in question did not live up to its ideals and cannot be considered binding on either partner. It makes no statement about the children and in no way confers on them a status of illegitimacy.

If you still decide against an annulment, however, the answer to your question is no. The Catholic Church can only celebrate the marriage of people free to marry. To establish your freedom, you will need an annulment. Please give it a try.

---

11. *May the Catholic Church give me a quick marriage without a ceremony? I just want to make the relationship legal before I go into the service.*

The only kind of marriage we witness is one in the context of a worship service. If you just want to pick up a marriage license, say "I do," and leave—then no, we cannot help you.

In case of an emergency, we need only the exchange of consent before two witnesses (*Code of Canon Law* 1119), but your pastor would have to judge if you have an emergency here. Ordinarily, we put the ceremony in the midst of prayer including readings from Scripture and blessings for the couple.

Even that can be done simply and briefly, but we witness more than a legal marriage. We witness a spiritual marriage.

12. *I'm a Catholic. Does my fiancé have to become a Catholic to be married in the church?*

No, not at all. Many people think this is true, but it is not. Of course, if your fiancé would like to become a Catholic or to learn more about your church, your parish will be glad to help. But it is not a prerequisite for marriage.

13. My partner has never been baptized. May we still get married?

Yes, indeed. We have a special ceremony for the marriage between a Catholic and an unbaptized person. It differs only slightly from the wedding between a Catholic and another baptized person.

For example, the ceremony is supposed to take place outside of Mass (*Rite of Marriage* 8). It will be like attending the first half of Mass, including the Scripture readings. The marriage ceremony follows the readings, and then you receive a blessing, offer some prayers, and conclude.

The rite of marriage between a Catholic and an unbaptized person excludes references to "the sacrament of marriage." This marriage is considered valid—it "counts"—but is not a sacrament. The sacraments are our deepest celebrations of the presence of Christ. The first sacrament, baptism, opens the door to participating in the others. An unbaptized person does not participate in sacraments as the baptized do. The marriage of two people may be a sacrament only if both are baptized. If one partner is not baptized, the marriage is not a sacrament. But it would still be considered Catholic and valid.

If at any point in the marriage your partner becomes baptized, the action makes your marriage a sacrament. Your marriage to an unbaptized person is still a Catholic wedding, still a union that lasts forever. It just does not have the quality of the sacrament that exists when Christ is made present in the marriage of two baptized partners.

14. We're not Catholic, but the person I'm marrying is preparing to become one. May we get married in the Catholic Church?

Yes, you may. If you are both baptized, you will celebrate the sacrament of marriage in a Catholic ceremony. It will probably not include Mass, because neither of you is eligible for communion in the Catholic Church.

If you are engaged to a catechumen, you may have that marriage in the Catholic Church as well. A catechumen is an unbaptized adult preparing for baptism in the Catholic Church. That catechumen may marry anyone—baptized or unbaptized—in a Catholic ceremony. The marriage will not be considered a sacrament until both partners are baptized, but it will be a valid marriage—one that counts—from the very beginning.

15. *We want our marriage to last forever but we are signing a legal agreement concerning our property just in case it doesn't. Will this be a problem?*

Could be. Marriage is indissoluble (*Code of Canon Law* 1056). If there is doubt about your intentions to enter a permanent union, the pastor will not be able to authorize the ceremony. If you have signed a legal document of this nature, you may be giving evidence that you are not entering this marriage with full intent for it to last forever. That means you want something different from what the Catholic Church offers: indissoluble marriage.

16. My partner is under 18. Do parents have to consent to this marriage?

Possibly, but it depends on where you live.

The Catholic Church cannot be involved with the marriage of people below the legal age for marriage (*Code of Canon Law* 1072), so the first factor is to observe the local civil laws. A "minor child" may marry if the parents are aware of it and not reasonably opposed to it (c. 1071/6).

As far as the church is concerned and if civil law is no different, the minimum age for marriage is 16 for men and 14 for women (c. 1083). A conference of bishops may raise those ages.

Consequently, some testimony from the parents of an 18-year old may be necessary, depending on the local legislation. Ask your parish minister about this.

17. *My homosexual partner and I want our union to last forever. May we have a ceremony in the Catholic Church?*

Not the kind you would like. Marriage in the Catholic Church requires a man and a woman (*Code of Canon Law* 1057/2). We do not have any other kind of commitment ceremony for couples.

We do have some generic blessings at the end of the *Book of Blessings*, and one of these could legitimately be used over individuals or friends. For example, chapter 71 contains the "Order for a Blessing to Be Used in Various Circumstances." Numbers 2004–2008 offer several blessings for the special occasions of life. But they should not be misconstrued as a wedding.

The church explicitly calls homosexual persons to chastity (*Catechism of the Catholic Church* 2359), even while it stresses they "must be accepted with respect, compassion, and sensitivity" (2358).

18. *Do we have to agree to raise our kids Catholic before we may get married? Even though I'm Catholic, I'd like the children raised in my partner's faith.*

Catholic parties are asked to do "all in their power" to baptize and raise their children in the Catholic faith (*Code of Canon Law* 1136). A Catholic marrying a person of another faith will make this promise orally or in writing, and the other party needs only be informed of the Catholic's responsibility (*Directory for the Application on Principals and Norms on Ecumenism* 150). In this way Catholics demonstrate their love for the church and their desire to share it with the children they love as well. If you love your family, your heritage, your neighborhood, or your political party, you will want to share these with your children. The church assumes you will also want to share your faith.

There are circumstances in which the Catholic party meets opposition from the spouse. It is for those reasons that we understand Catholics will do "all in their power" to fulfill this responsibility. Sometimes it will not be possible.

In your case, however, it appears that your commitment to your church is less than your partner's. Search more deeply in your soul. You are asking for a Catholic wedding. Does that represent a true love for the church that you would like to share with your children? Or are you having a Catholic wedding to please someone else when your own heart is not in it?

19. My fiancé and I don't want kids. Is that going to be a problem?

Yes, that will be a problem. Marriage is "ordered toward the good of the spouses and the procreation and education of offspring" (*Code of Canon Law* 1055). If you are designing your marriage to be childless, you are choosing a relationship that is different from what the Catholic Church understands marriage to be: a union ordered toward offspring. A Catholic pastor will not be able to authorize a wedding for a couple who are excluding children. In fact, if such a couple were to divorce, the church could grant an annulment of the marriage on these grounds.

Ask yourselves what you would do if you discovered, in spite of your intent, that you were expecting a baby. Would you welcome that child to your family? If so, you probably do not completely desire the exclusion of children, and you might be eligible for a Catholic wedding. Help the pastor make a good judgment.

20. We are too old to have children. May we still get married in the church?

Yes, you may. "Sterility neither prohibits nor invalidates marriage" (*Code of Canon Law* 1084/3). Childless spouses can have a meaningful married life. "Their marriage can radiate a fruitfulness of charity, of hospitality, and of sacrifice" (*Catechism of the Catholic Church* 1654).

21. *I don't like my parish church. May I get married at some other one?*

It depends. The church presumes that the marriage will take place in the parish church of the Catholic bride or groom (*Code of Canon Law* 1115). But there are exceptions. The bishop or pastor may permit the marriage to take place somewhere else.

A lot of couples presume they pick a church like they pick a reception hall. For Catholics, this is different. Ordinarily the wedding is to take place in the Catholic church of the bride or groom.

This preference exists because of the relationship of individuals to the parish community. Parishes exist for the spiritual benefit of the faithful. It is there you celebrate the Sunday Eucharist, have opportunities for education, experience forgiveness, and render service to the community. Your parish should be the logical place for a wedding to occur.

Some people prefer another parish church because they do not like the appearance of their own or they want something more convenient for the reception. But the parish holds significance in the life of its members. If you are looking for some other church for the wedding, ask yourself how much of a commitment you have made to your parish community. Your search may be a signal that you have not made the connections with the faith community that calls that house of worship its home.

If you still want the wedding somewhere else, your pastor will have to approve it, so start with him.

22. I don't like my pastor. May someone else do the wedding?

Yes, but only with your pastor's permission. Your pastor has jurisdiction over your wedding. Even if you have never met him, he is responsible for the event.

If some other priest is to preside for the wedding, your pastor will have to delegate him (*Code of Canon Law* 1111). Pastors do this either orally or in writing, depending on local custom. Most will allow someone else to come in for the honors.

However, finding another priest can be more difficult than you think. Many priests have very hectic weekends and are not able to freelance for weddings at locations other than their own. If you invite another priest to preside for your wedding, be prepared he might have to say no.

By the way, any priest or deacon working at your parish may already have the faculty (the bishop's permission) to witness marriages there. If your parish has more clergy besides the pastor, you may ask one of them for assistance.

23. *Did you say a deacon could perform the ceremony?*

Yes. A deacon ordained for the Catholic Church may witness weddings. He just needs the pastor to give him delegation for your ceremony. Obviously, the wedding will be a church service without Mass, because deacons do not preside at the Eucharist. But it will be a bona fide Catholic wedding.

24. I'm Catholic, but I don't belong to a Catholic parish. How can I get married in the Catholic Church?

You may not realize this, but you do belong to a Catholic parish. All our parishes are territorial and we have all the territory covered. You are within the boundaries of some parish, wherever you live. That pastor has responsibility for your wedding.

You can find out what parish you are in by calling any Catholic church in the area, or the chancery office, or diocesan center. Many dioceses and parishes have websites.

Some pastors will help you right away. Others may want you to be active in the community for a while before they will arrange the wedding. If the pastor has never seen you before, your first meeting could be uncomfortable. But check it out and ask for help. Ultimately, pastors want to serve the people of God, and you are one of them. Yours will do what he can. If you feel like the pastor of the place where you live is not helping you enough, contact the office of the local bishop and ask for advice.

25. My fiancé is not a Catholic. May we be married at his or her church?

Yes, but only with good reason and with the proper procedures. For example, if your fiancé is very active in another religion, has a conscientious objection to a Catholic wedding, or even has family members who object to a Catholic service, you may request permission from your Catholic pastor to have the wedding witnessed by your fiancé's pastor at his or her church. Your pastor will submit a written request for the dispensation, and the bishop of the diocese will approve it (*Code of Canon Law* 1127/2). When this happens, you will have obtained a dispensation from canonical form. This means the wedding of you, the Catholic, does not have to be witnessed by a Catholic minister inside a Catholic church. Many people assume that a Catholic priest or deacon must be present at such a service for it to count as a valid Catholic wedding. That is not so. Once the dispensation from form is granted, your fiancé's minister becomes the official witness of a marriage that the Catholic Church will recognize as a valid marriage.

If you want your Catholic priest or deacon to witness your marriage in your fiancé's place of worship, he may or may not be able to do so depending on the policies of the diocese. And if that building is in the boundaries of another parish, your pastor may need delegation from the pastor of that parish, as well as the bishop's permission. It's complicated, but in some dioceses it may be done.

26. I'm Catholic, but I don't go to church. May we still have a Catholic wedding?

Theoretically, yes, but practically it will depend on your pastor. He makes the judgment about your readiness for marriage. If he thinks that your decision not to participate in the Sunday Eucharist constitutes a serious obstacle to your spiritual preparation for marriage, he may tell you so. It depends on why you do not attend church.

Think about this for a minute, though. If there is one single, basic, fundamental activity that lies at the heart of Catholic identity and behavior, it is the Eucharist. If participation at Sunday Mass is not part of your life, you are missing out on the very core of what it is to be a Catholic. If there is one piece of Catholic behavior you should have in place, it is not learning how to prepare for a Catholic wedding. It is participation at the Eucharist.

27. I'm Catholic, but I haven't been confirmed yet. May I still get married?

Theoretically, yes, but practically it will depend. Catholics should be confirmed before marriage "if they can do so without serious inconvenience" (*Code of Canon Law* 1065).

That law was written for the sake of people in parts of the world where confirmations are rare because bishops are few in a territory that is vast. If you have grown up in an environment where you had ample opportunity to present yourself for confirmation and did not, this is a good time to arrange it.

Confirmation is the gift of the Holy Spirit that directs the baptized toward mission in the church. It fills you with strength so that you may live the Christian life more faithfully.

Although the *Code of Canon Law* does not absolutely require confirmation before someone can be married, there are dioceses and pastors who do. Check this out with your local parish. And if you have not yet been confirmed, ask how you might prepare yourself for this sacrament.

28. *I'm Catholic, but I never had my first communion. May I still get married?*

Y ou are not required to have first communion before marriage, so yes it is possible.

But, ask at the parish where you are preparing for marriage if its staff can arrange the preparation for your communion as well. You will find participation in the Eucharist to be an excellent spiritual preparation for marriage (*Code of Canon Law* 1065/2).

> **29.** My spouse and I weren't married in a Catholic church but we realize now that we should have. What do we do?

Visit your pastor. He will help you prepare and celebrate a Catholic marriage.

If you are a Catholic, the law of the church binds you to the Catholic form of marriage (*Code of Canon Law* 1117). If you got married but did not have a Catholic service and did not obtain a dispensation from canonical form through your Catholic pastor, the Catholic Church does not recognize your marriage. You are asked to abstain from the Eucharist while you are in this situation.

You may be able to square this away very easily. The pastor may have an uncomplicated process of preparation. To have your marriage recognized by the church, or "convalidated," he will celebrate the Catholic rite of marriage with you. Most people do this very simply in the presence of a few family members and friends.

If one of you is not a Catholic and objects to having the ceremony again, ask your pastor about a sanation. In some cases he can convalidate the marriage on paper without a ceremony (c. 1161).

If one of you has a previous marriage, you will need to obtain an annulment first. Again, your pastor should be able to help you manage all these steps.

Please give this some thought. You will find many spiritual benefits from having your marriage celebrated in the Catholic Church.

30. Can two marriages happen at the same ceremony? We have two engagements in the family.

Yes, we can celebrate multiple marriages in the same ceremony. In some countries, especially mission regions, this is common because of the infrequent visits of the Catholic clergy. This situation is covered in the Catholic Church's *Rite of Marriage*.

> **31.** We're planning to elope. How do I get the Catholic Church to bless our wedding next month?

You may find this next to impossible to accomplish. Pastors want to make sure that engaged couples are properly prepared for marriage. If you are planning a short engagement, you raise a question about how well you have thought through the decision to marry.

Remember, it is your Catholic pastor who has to approve your decision to marry. If you can convince him this is the right thing, he might arrange the ceremony. But most will not. You could call around searching for some priest to help, and you might find one, but he will be bending the rules if he witnesses this marriage without the permission of your pastor.

Preparing
The Ceremony

32. *Is there a waiting period to get married? I've heard you have to wait six months.*

There is usually a waiting period. The universal law of the church does not designate one, but many dioceses have a minimum requirement of six months. Some make it less, but others make it more. During that time, the parish typically will offer you sessions of marriage preparation.

For many couples, this is no longer a surprise nor an inconvenience. Weddings take a long time to organize. Many reception halls have to be booked much earlier than six months before the wedding. Just be sure to contact your parish as soon as you announce the engagement.

33. How come we have to go to classes before we can get married, what are they all about, and how long do they last?

The classes are intended to help you make a thoughtful preparation for marriage. Your minds will be filled with details about the wedding. Your parish will want to help you think about the marriage.

The sessions usually include topics like communication, conflict resolution, financial management, sexuality, and spirituality. The content and quality of these sessions varies considerably from one parish to another. A married couple from your community will probably lead them. Be assured that the church has your best interests at heart and sincerely wants to help you make your engagement period a special time. The church also wants to help you create a marriage that will last. Many couples go into these sessions wishing they could do something else, but finish them very grateful for what they learned.

The length of the preparation varies. You can often complete the preparation within a couple of months, but most parishes want about six months' notice to give them ample time to complete the series.

In some cases, parishes will not reserve your date for the wedding until you have completed your preparation. Some dioceses require this to make sure you will attend the sessions, causing couples to feel like they are mistrusted and penalized. Ideally, the preparation should not cause antagonism. It should help build a solid marriage in Christ.

34. Do the classes include religious instruction for a partner who is not Catholic?

They should, but they do not always. A partner who is not Catholic will probably want to know some things about the Catholic Church, and the parish should be ready to provide the information. To marry a Catholic, your fiancé does not have to show any interest in becoming a Catholic, but the parish should show some interest in keeping your partner informed.

35. *If my partner refuses to attend the classes or skips some of them, may we still get married in the church?*

Check with your pastor as this is a judgment call. Ordinarily, we hope for goodwill between the couple and the parish. If your partner has a sincere, conscientious reason for not attending the sessions, you should discuss this with your pastor. If your partner is just being stubborn, that's another matter. The sessions are designed for your benefit. You want a successful marriage. Your parish wants the same for you.

36. My fiancé and I live in two different cities. How can we possibly take classes together?

If you can arrange it, it is better for the two of you to attend the sessions together. Many parishes will make accommodations with their schedule by offering a series of weekend sessions, a single weekend retreat, or some days over a holiday break. This is your marriage we're talking about, so it is worth the time, expense, and effort for you to spend the preparation time of your engagement together.

If it is completely impossible to take the preparation together, talk with your pastor and negotiate another option. Perhaps you can each do the sessions where you live and share notes by phone or e-mail. But try to do something significant to prepare your hearts for a faithful marriage.

37. Why do Catholics get married at Mass? It takes so long.

Marriage is one of the seven sacraments of the Catholic Church. The permanent love of husband and wife signifies the love that God has for the church. Marriage is a covenant in which two parties agree to go out of their way to be with the other, just as God does in the divine covenant with us. We celebrate marriage at Mass to show the connection between this loving relationship of partners and the loving relationship we all share with God. This divine love reaches its most beautiful expression in our celebration of the Eucharist. There we experience our complete union with God, through the Body and Blood of Christ.

Yes, it takes a long time for a Catholic wedding. But it takes a while to enter into its spirit of prayer. And once you are truly there, you won't want to leave.

38. *We just want a simple ceremony. Maybe just the vows. Or the wedding and communion. Is that possible with the Catholic Church or do we have to have Mass?*

Catholic marriage does not have to take place at Mass. When the partners come from two different faiths, it is often a good idea to have the ceremony apart from Mass. In that case, you have the procession, the Scriptures, the marriage ceremony, the blessings, and the conclusion of the ceremony. Depending on how much music and ceremony it includes, a Catholic wedding without Mass can still take half an hour or so. (You never get out quickly in a Catholic wedding.)

The wedding can be done simply, but it should include these elements. We do not offer a ceremony only with vows, or just the wedding part and communion. Scripture readings are an essential part of the celebration. There is a format for weddings without a Mass in the *Rite of Marriage*, available at every Catholic parish on the planet. Your pastor will have a copy and will know how it goes.

Marriage without Mass is still a valid Catholic wedding. There is no difference in the end result, with or without Mass. You will be married in the church.

39. *If a Catholic marries someone from another faith, are they forbidden to have Mass with the ceremony?*

If the Catholic marries someone who is unbaptized, the ceremony takes place apart from Mass. Otherwise Mass is optional. According to an old tradition, the unbaptized, in preparation for becoming Christians, left the service after the Scriptures and before communion. Today many parishes observe the same custom with their catechumens. Because the unbaptized are ineligible for communion, they leave after the homily to reflect more deeply on the Scriptures.

Your parish or diocese may have special regulations about the wedding Mass. For example, priests are not supposed to preside for more than three Masses in one day (*Code of Canon Law* 905). If a wedding comes on a weekend when he already has other Masses scheduled, he may propose that the ceremony not include Mass. Ask your pastor for the pros and cons of marriage with Mass.

40. Is the wedding still a sacrament if there is no Mass?

Yes, the wedding is still a sacrament as long as both parties are baptized. The Mass does not make the marriage a sacrament. The people do.

Oftentimes it is the Catholic parents who fear embarrassment if their child is married without a Mass. But a ceremony without Mass may be more hospitable to the couple and the guests. The marriage still counts.

41. Will my Saturday wedding count for Sunday Mass?

If your wedding takes place on a Saturday evening in the context of Mass, it will count for Sunday.

Even many priests do not understand this. Catholics are obliged to attend Mass on Sunday, but any Mass fulfills this obligation. It does not have to be a regularly scheduled Sunday Mass. Some priests have announced at the wedding that they are giving permission for this ceremony to count for Sunday. That permission is not theirs to give. The law of the church already gave it (*Code of Canon Law* 1248/1).

However, if your wedding does not include Mass, it obviously does not count for Sunday Mass. The church expects Catholics to come back over the weekend for the Eucharist.

Moreover, the law of the church does not further specify what is "Saturday evening." This becomes another judgment call. If the wedding takes place in the morning or early Saturday afternoon, it does not count for Sunday because you are celebrating too early in the day. Check the time of the parish Saturday evening Mass. If your wedding takes place around that time or later, you can be sure it is "Saturday evening."

Be careful, though. Some parishes and dioceses do not permit the celebration of marriage with a Mass on a Saturday evening. So ask about this at your parish.

42. May I get married on some other day of the week?

Yes, you may get married on any day of the week. It does not have to be a Saturday to get married in the Catholic Church.

However, you may not get married on Good Friday or Holy Saturday as we do not celebrate the sacraments on those days.

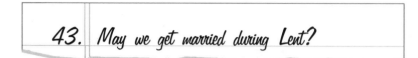

43. May we get married during Lent?

Yes. The answer used to be no, but the current legislation permits weddings during Lent.

Still, there are things you should know. Advent and Lent are considered times of penance, and the priest is supposed to advise you to take this into consideration when planning your ceremony (*Rite of Marriage* 11).

If your wedding takes place with a Mass on a Saturday night or Sunday during Lent, the prayers and readings should be taken from the Mass of that Sunday, not from the wedding Mass. You may, however, replace one of the readings with one from those recommended for weddings (11).

44. May we have two ceremonies — one Catholic and the other not? I've heard they do this in other countries, but that in the United States a Catholic who has a civil ceremony may not get married in the church.

You may not have two ceremonies (*Code of Canon Law* 1127/3). It is true that this is required in some countries where the church's minister is not recognized by the state. But in the United States your civil union and your spiritual union happen at the same event. There is to be no distinction and no question about whether or not you are married when the ceremony is over.

45. We're getting married outside the United States. Is the Catholic wedding ceremony different in other countries?

The basic ceremony is the same. Many countries have special traditions for weddings, and some of these will be incorporated into the Catholic ceremony. But the basic ritual is fundamentally the same everywhere in the world. All Catholic wedding ceremonies are based on the same original text.

46. *I'm supposed to plan my wedding ceremony and I don't have a clue. What are the contents of a Catholic wedding?*

Most of the planning is already done for you. The official book that describes the Catholic wedding is called the *Rite of Marriage*. There should be a copy of it in every Catholic church building. Other publications excerpt a selection of the prayers and Scripture readings from that book. The flow of the wedding ceremony is already set.

Visit with your priest or deacon about what you are supposed to plan. The *Rite of Marriage* includes options for the Scripture readings and the prayers the presider says, including the nuptial blessing. Ordinarily the presider will invite you to select the Scripture readings from the pool of those recommended for weddings. You might also choose from the optional prayer texts that he will say, but you will find that the nuances among those prayers are small compared with the more pronounced variety among the Scriptures.

If your wedding includes Mass, the parts of the ceremony are the procession, the Liturgy of the Word, the Rite of Marriage, and the Liturgy of the Eucharist. Without Mass, you omit the Liturgy of the Eucharist and have the conclusion of the ceremony.

47. What Bible readings are good for a wedding?

The *Rite of Marriage* recommends the following pool of readings from which you may choose:

Old Testament	New Testament	Psalm	Gospel
Genesis 1:26–28, 31a	Romans 8:31b–35, 37–39	33:12 and 18, 20–21, 22	Matthew 5:1–12
Genesis 2:18–24	Romans 12:1–2, 9–18 (longer) or Romans 12:1–2, 9–13 (shorter)	34:2–3, 4–5, 6–7, 8–9	Matthew 5:13–16
Genesis 24:48–51, 58–67	1 Corinthians 6:13c–15a, 17–20	103:1–2, 8 and 13, 17–18a	Matthew 7:21, 24–29 (longer) or 21, 24–25 (shorter)
Tobit 7:9–10, 11–15	1 Corinthians 12:31–13:8a	112:1–2, 3–4, 5–7a, 7bc–8, 9	Matthew 19:3–6
Tobit 8:5–10	Ephesians 5:2a, 21–33 (longer) or 2a, 25–32 (shorter)	128:1–2, 3, 4–5	Matthew 22:35–40
Song of Songs 2:8–10, 14, 16a; 8:6–7a	Colossians 3:12–17	145:8–9, 10 and 15, 17–18	Mark 10:6–9
Ecclesiasticus 26:1–4, 16–21 (Greek 1–4, 13–16)	1 Peter 3:1–9	148:1–2, 3–4, 9–10, 11–12ab, 12c–14a	John 2:1–11
Jeremiah 31:31–32a, 33–34a	1 John 3:18–24		John 15:9–12
	1 John 4:7–12		John 15:12–16
	Revelation 19:1, 5–9a		John 17:20–26 (longer) or 20–23 (shorter)

If you are picking readings for your wedding, follow these guidelines.

- Pick one from the Gospel column.

- Pick another from either the Old Testament or the New Testament column *or* one each from both these columns, in addition to your Gospel.

- Pick a psalm to be sung after the first reading.

There are some exceptions (RM 11).

- If your wedding includes a Mass and if it takes place on Holy Thursday, Easter, Christmas, Epiphany, Ascension, Pentecost, Corpus Christi, or on a holyday of obligation (in the United States these include January 1, August 15, November 1, and December 8), you must use all the Scripture readings of that day. None of the readings from the wedding Mass are to be used. To find out what those Scriptures are, check with your parish.

- If your wedding includes a Mass and if it takes place on a Saturday night or Sunday during the Advent, Lent, or Easter seasons, you should use the readings from that Sunday, but you may substitute one of them with one reading from the wedding Mass.

On all the other Saturday nights of the year, you may substitute all the Sunday Mass readings with those for a wedding.

If your wedding does not include Mass, you may choose any Scriptures from the chart above for any day.

48. *May we include some readings that are not from the Bible?*

Not during the Liturgy of the Word. This first part of the ceremony is when we listen to the inspired word of God. If you have other texts that are important to you, consider including them in your printed program. Depending on the text, your presider might suggest it be read during some other part of the ceremony.

But remember, people will be hearing many words during this wedding. As a church community, we'd like the word of God to stand out.

49. What should go into the program?

The program should help the people gathered together for your wedding to participate. They come to a Catholic wedding not just to watch but to be active witnesses to the event. They will join in prayer for you and in praise of God.

The program should contain a basic outline of the service: entrance rites, Liturgy of the Word, Rite of Marriage, and Liturgy of the Eucharist, if your wedding includes a Mass.

It may also include the titles of the music for the ceremony. Reference the music the assembly will sing if it is to be found in hymnals or other participation aids. If you reproduce music in your wedding booklet, be sure to secure permission from the copyright owner of each piece.

You may also include the names of the people who will play a leading role in the service. List names of the people in the order of the procession so those attending can tell who is who.

Include a line in the program reminding people to turn off their cell phones and pagers.

If you are expecting people who do not regularly attend the Catholic Mass, include the spoken responses they are expected to make, like "Lord, have mercy" in the penitential rite, "Thanks be to God" after the readings, "Praise to you, Lord Jesus Christ" after the Gospel, "Amen" during the blessing of the rings, and "Lord, hear our prayer" for the prayer of the faithful. If the wedding includes a Mass, the program should include: the Nicene Creed if it is a Mass for Sunday, "Blessed be God forever" and "May the Lord receive this sacrifice at your hands for the praise and glory of his name, for our good, and the good of all his Church" during the prayer over the gifts, the preface dialogue and "Holy, Holy, Holy," memorial acclamation and "Amen" during the eucharistic prayer, the Lord's Prayer, the sign of peace, "Lord I am not worthy to receive you, but only say the word and I shall be healed" at communion, "Amen" for the blessings, and "Thanks be to God" for the dismissals. These texts are copyrighted by the International Committee on English in the Liturgy, Inc., Washington D.C.

You may obtain permission from that office for the reprints (see bibliography).

Do your parish a favor by including some basic information about the church in the program such as the address, phone number, and website. The program might even include something about the community the parish serves, the patron saint, or upcoming events.

Show the program to a parish minister before it goes to press and invite some additional ideas.

50. Are there restrictions on decorations?

Check with your parish. Many parishes will ask you to respect the decorations already in place for the season. They may have specific rules about the placement of candles and flowers.

During the season of Lent, we usually try to keep decorations minimal, in the spirit of the season. It would help the local community if your wedding decorations did not overpower the sense of the season of the year.

51. Does it matter how we dress?

Dress for weddings is a matter of social custom. The church makes no requirements about how people dress, except for the liturgical ministers such as your presider.

Nonetheless, yes, it matters how you dress. Remember this is a church service, and the event is formal. What you wear should not distract people from worship. Please be sensitive to the needs of your guests to experience this wedding in this church as a complete setting for prayer.

Some brides wear a veil. Others do not. The veil is not part of the Catholic liturgy, so it is completely optional.

The church usually provides a place where the bride and bridesmaids may dress, but be sure to ask about this ahead of time. Visit the space so you have a sense of what it provides and what it lacks. Ask how long this location is available to you on the wedding day. You may need to vacate it shortly after the wedding. The church might need it for another function, or the entire building may need to be locked. Do not count on leaving things here to be picked up later.

You should not feel under any obligation to spend money on clothes you cannot afford. The poor are also entitled to weddings. We do not expect anyone to dress beyond their means.

52. What music is appropriate at weddings?

The music should serve the wedding liturgy. The rules governing what music you may use vary considerably from parish to parish. Some have no regulations. Others have strict guidelines. Be sure to ask before you plan the music.

First consider the music of the service. Give the assembly something to sing so they can make their praise of God heard. Include a responsorial psalm and a Gospel acclamation. If your wedding includes a Mass, all should sing the acclamations during the eucharistic prayer and all should sing a processional song during communion.

You may have a cantor lead the singing, and you may have solos sung. But the heart of wedding music should not be the solos. It should be the music that involves the people in the liturgy. The Lord's Prayer, for example, is a prayer recited or sung by all who gather for worship. It is not appropriate for a soloist to take that prayer away from the people and sing it alone.

Some of the music you like may have come from secular sources. Many parishes will ask you not to include these in the wedding ceremony. Your wedding liturgy is like any other gathering of the faithful in this church. Songs made famous in the movies and on the radio are not usually sung when we gather to worship on Sunday—before, during, or after the service. We sing the songs of worship. You will help the parish if you start to think about selecting wedding music from the music you ordinarily hear at church.

For similar reasons, it is best not use recorded music as part of the ceremony. People have come to worship, not to listen to the greatest hits. Many couples appropriately use recorded music at the reception.

Some parishes prefer you use their musicians. Be sure to ask for the local rules.

53. What rules are there about photography?

These rules will vary from place to place, too. Be sure to ask your parish if there is a photography policy. Then communicate it to the photographer you hire.

Most photographers want to observe the local rules, so the clearer things are ahead of time the smoother the ceremony will proceed.

Be aware the parish may need to use the church before or after your wedding, limiting the time when photos may be taken. Confessions, Masses, or other weddings may compete for the time the church is available. Many photographers will want as much of your time as they can get to multiply the photos from which you may choose. Be sure you know when the parish needs to have the building clear again.

The parish may have local policies about video cameras as well. A few are equipped with installed video equipment, ready to record any church service.

54. *My partner is not Catholic. May a minister from that church and my priest co-officiate the wedding?*

To some extent, yes, but they are not exactly equals. It should be clear who the main presider is for the ceremony, and who will ask and receive your consent (the vows). If your fiancé's minister belongs to another faith, either that minister or the Catholic one may serve as the official witness, but not both. They cannot each do their own ritual in the same ceremony (*Code of Canon Law* 1127/3). The Catholic minister may not ask for the consent of the Catholic party while the other minister asks the consent of the other party. It needs to be very clear from the perspective of both church and state just who the minister is who officially witnesses the wedding. If the other minister asks and receives the consent of the couple, the Catholic party must first obtain from his or her pastor a dispensation from canonical form (c. 1127/2).

If the wedding takes place at your partner's place of worship, a Catholic priest or deacon may assist at the invitation of that minister. The Catholic minister should not ask for and receive the consent, but "may offer other appropriate prayers, read from the Scriptures, give a brief exhortation and bless the couple" (*Directory for the Application on Principals and Norms on Ecumenism* 157).

If you want the other minister to come to the Catholic parish to assist, the bishop may permit your priest to invite that minister "to participate in the celebration of the marriage, to read from the Scriptures, give a brief exhortation and bless the couple" (DAPNE 158).

55. *I have lots of family and friends I want to involve in the wedding. What can they do?*

There are lots of possibilities.

- Ushers: It is a courtesy to have ushers welcome the guests and help them find a seat especially for those unfamiliar with your church. They should act like greeters, making people feel at home. Oddly, some couples have ushers seat friends of the bride on one side and friends of the groom on the other. Many couples now avoid separating the guests.

- Servers: Whether or not your ceremony includes a Mass, your presider may need the assistance of altar servers to hold the ritual book, carry candles in procession, and perform other server functions. The parish will probably have its own servers and some presiders prefer them because they know the routine. The server can assist in the smooth execution of the service, but an untrained server will cause more chaos than order.

- Candlelighters: The Catholic ceremony does not specifically call for a ritual lighting of candles. Many weddings include it, but it is not part of the ceremony. You may have someone light candles before the procession if you wish, but our tradition is to have servers light them informally as people enter the building.

- Flower girls and ring bearers: These traditional roles do not appear in the Catholic *Rite of Marriage*, but many couples include them in the procession. The most common blunder to avoid is choosing children who are too young. Confusion can spoil cuteness.

- Attendants: You may have family and friends join the procession and take honorary positions up front. The most common problem here is recruiting too many attendants. Some parishes have restrictions, so be sure to ask. The primary symbols of the wedding are the bride and groom, and they should not be swallowed in a sea of attendants.

- Readers: Reading the word of God is an important part of the ceremony. Entrust this task to someone with experience as a reader in a church. The job is harder than it appears to be.

- Gift bearers: If your wedding includes a Mass, you may have someone bring gifts to the altar. These "gifts" are the bread and wine for the mass—not your wedding gifts. Gifts for the poor and the church may also be brought up if you and the guests are making an offering in conjunction with your wedding. There is no rule about people who belong to other faiths bringing up the gifts. But as Catholics are the only ones who will be receiving communion at the Mass, it is a little rude to have someone who is not Catholic bring up the bread and wine on behalf of the community, when they will be excluded from sharing these gifts later in the service. The symbol works better if Catholics bring up the gifts.

- Communion ministers: If your wedding includes a Mass, be sure you have ample communion ministers to offer communion under both forms. They should visit with the priest beforehand so they know what to do. If you do not know enough communion ministers, your priest may invite some from the parish, or he may even appoint some of your family and friends to be communion ministers for this one ceremony (*Sacramentary*, Appendix V).

- The assembly: Don't forget that the people who come to your wedding are not just "guests". They are the assembly of the faithful. They are ministers. Each of them has a role to play in singing, praying, and witnessing this event.

56. *Children are already involved in our relationship. May they have a role in the wedding?*

Yes, and you may talk with your presider about the possibilities. There is no clear role for the couple's children in the Rite of Marriage, but they may appropriately assume one. The *Book of Blessings* (IV) and *Catholic Household Blessings and Prayers* (page 226) include blessings for children that could be incorporated into the ceremony.

But remember that the wedding is primarily about the two people exchanging their consent. The bride and groom need to stand out as the central figures. A blessing of children might be appropriate among the blessings that conclude the wedding.

57. *What roles could my partner and I play?*
May we be communion ministers
at the wedding?

You may, but think about this: Your primary role is to be the ministers of marriage. You give your consent to each other and the rest of us are witnesses. You already have a huge role to play.

However, if you are communion ministers in your church, there is no rule forbidding you to assume that ministry at the wedding.

Another ministry to consider would be greeter. Some couples stand by the door of the church and greet the members of the assembly as they arrive. It just depends on your personality and gifts.

58. Do the best man and maid of honor have to be Catholic?

No, they do not. You just need any two witnesses besides the presider (*Code of Canon Law* 1108/1). They should be able to comprehend what is going on, so they need to be at the age of the use of reason. If their comprehension is impaired, for example, by intoxication, they may not serve.

But they need not be Catholic. In fact, they do not even have to be baptized. They are witnesses to the event (*Directory for the Application on Principals and Norms on Ecumenism* 136).

> **59.** *The best man and maid of honor are the traditional witnesses, but we want to have two witnesses of the same sex. Is this allowed?*

Yes, this is allowed. There is no church law that says the two witnesses have to be of two sexes.

60. Does the Scripture reader have to be Catholic?

If your wedding takes place at Mass, the Scripture reader needs to be Catholic or a member of one of the Eastern rites (*Directory for the Application on Principals and Norms on Ecumenism* 126, 133). If you want someone from another faith to read at the wedding Mass, you actually need permission from the bishop (133).

If the wedding is not a Mass, anyone may read (135, 118).

61. What will happen at the wedding rehearsal?

The rehearsal should help the wedding party prepare for the ceremony.

Impress on everyone the importance of being prompt. Whoever leads the rehearsal will want to get started on time, and if some are late it will impair the success of the rehearsal.

You will probably practice the procession in and the procession out. They are the most difficult parts of the ceremony to coordinate. In addition, you may need some direction about where to stand and what to do during the Rite of Marriage itself.

The rehearsal may include prayer. This will bless your efforts and help everyone remember the seriousness of the ceremony. Sometimes the priest will be available to celebrate the sacrament of reconciliation.

You may also invite the readers to rehearse. This will allow them to try out the microphone and to go over the Scriptures out loud.

62. What paperwork has to be completed before the wedding?

Before the wedding, the pastor will need the following documents and information to complete the paperwork.

Catholics need to supply a newly issued copy of their baptismal certificate. If your parents have your original stuffed into a shoebox in the closet of their home, you cannot use it. You need a new one from the Catholic parish where you were baptized (or received into the full communion of the Catholic Church). Parishes get these requests all the time. Contact your first parish church, tell them you're planning to get married, and ask them to send you or the parish the new certificate.

The reason it has to be new is that the church of your baptism (or reception) contains your permanent records as a Catholic. After you are married, a record of your wedding will be sent to that church, and they will make a notation of your wedding in your baptismal record.

When you request a new copy of the baptismal certificate, the parish holding the records will update the information and issue it to you. Your new certificate will show you all the records currently on file at the church of your baptism.

So, if your Catholic fiancé has been concealing another marriage all these years, you will find out about it when the baptismal certificate arrives.

You will also need to supply the appropriate decrees if there are any previous marriages, divorces, annulments, or deceased spouses.

A parish minister will then complete the official form registering your wedding. You will be asked questions such as where you live, whether you are a nun or a priest, your intentions to have children, whether you are confirmed, and your desire for a marriage that will last until you die. If any permissions or dispensations need to be granted (for example, concerning the place or minister of the wedding, or if a Catholic wishes to marry someone from another faith), they go with these papers as well.

The whole process is fairly painless, but it is a necessary step before a Catholic wedding may happen.

63. What are the banns of marriage?

The banns are public notices about an upcoming wedding. They are part of the church's inquiry to make sure that the parties are eligible for marriage (*Code of Canon Law* 1067). If someone wanting to get married is actually married already, the banns are supposed to catch it.

In the past, the banns were published three times in the parish bulletin, prior to the wedding. Today that is no longer required. And let's face it: publishing something in a parish bulletin guarantees a small reading audience. Some parishes, however, still publish the banns. Others do so not out of suspicion, but as a way of spreading the good news about your engagement.

64. Should I go to confession before I get married?

It would be a very good idea. The church strongly recommends the sacrament of reconciliation prior to marriage (*Code of Canon Law* 1065/2).

In truth, reconciliation is required only for those who have committed serious sin (988). Celebrating reconciliation is recommended for lesser sins. Still, the overall point of this sacrament is to seek a conversion of heart, an improvement in the spiritual life. It would be a gift to yourself, to your partner, and to the community for you to ask God's forgiveness for past misdeeds and to seek God's strength for the future.

As you plan the days before your wedding, reserve some time to confess your sins at church. If you don't schedule the time now, it will be too easy to find an excuse not to go when the wedding day draws near. Find out when confessions are scheduled or make an appointment with the priest. Experience God's forgiving love as you take this important step in your life.

The Ceremony

65. How is the procession supposed to go?

Y ou will never believe this, but the description of the procession in the Catholic *Rite of Marriage* is nothing like what usually happens.

> At the appointed time, the priest, vested for Mass, goes with the ministers to the door of the church or, if more suitable, to the altar. There he meets the bride and bridegroom in a friendly manner, showing that the Church shares their joy.
>
> Where it is desirable that the rite of welcome be omitted, the celebration of marriage begins at once with the Mass.
>
> If there is a procession to the altar, the ministers go first, followed by the priest, and then the bride and the bridegroom. According to local custom, they may be escorted by at least their parents and the two witnesses. Meanwhile, the entrance song is sung (19-20).

To interpret this text, remember that the primary ministers of the sacrament of marriage are you—the bride and groom, not the clergy. They do not marry you. You marry each other. The priest is a witness—the official witness of the church, but a witness just like the best man, maid of honor, ring bearer, mother of the bride, and the friend who bought the cheapest gift.

The *Rite of Marriage* envisions a welcome before the procession begins. The bride and groom are standing together near the door of the church. The presider goes there to say hello and how happy the church is for them. Most couples would never consider this welcoming because of the superstition that the bride and groom should not see each other before the wedding. The superstition, of course, is ridiculous.

The *Rite of Marriage* next describes a procession led by "the ministers followed by the priest." The ministers here are the servers and the reader. Your Scripture reader should be in the procession, just as you see at Mass on Sundays.

The bride and bridegroom follow the presider in the procession. At many weddings, you see something completely different. The bride comes up the aisle with her attendants, and the groom comes out the side door with his attendants showing they come from different backgrounds. The priest comes out a different door (because nobody knows where he comes from). Everyone converges at the altar and the ceremony begins. But the Catholic *Rite of Marriage* has something very different in mind. It actually envisions that the bride and groom come up the aisle together, that there is one procession for all who are involved in the ceremony, just as you would see at Mass on Sundays. The difference is that at a typical Eucharist, the main minister is the priest. But at a wedding, the main ministers are the bride and groom. That's why they come last in the procession.

The *Rite of Marriage* then states the couple may be escorted by at least their parents and the two witnesses. Note the plural: parents. It does not say "the bride is walked down the aisle by her father." The Catholic marriage rite assumes that if one parent is involved, all the others are too. Why should the groom's parents be omitted from the procession altogether? And although it mentions "at least the two witnesses"—meaning the best man and maid of honor—many couples multiply the number of witnesses in the wedding party. There is no rule against it, but the idea of the procession is that it will not be overly crowded and that the two principal people—the bride and groom—will stand out.

Envision the procession this way: Servers and Scripture reader go first, followed by the presider. Then your attendants walk down the same aisle. The parents all follow the attendants, and the bride and groom enter the church arm in arm. In an alternate form, following the attendants, the groom is escorted by his parents followed by the bride escorted by hers.

Your procession is going to send a message about what you believe in terms of equality of the partners and the importance of parental relationships. In the procession for your wedding, think about how you can best symbolize what you believe.

The *Rite of Marriage* makes no reference to a white runner down the center aisle. Although many churches use one anyway, others do not. In general, the wedding procession should resemble the procession that begins Mass. The runner may not be necessary.

66. Will the priest be asking, "Who gives this woman to this man?"

No. This is not part of the Catholic marriage rite. It happens on television, in movies, and in some churches in real life. But the Catholic rite does not include this question.

The question is way out of step with the times. It comes from a culture in which the father made arrangements for the daughter's wedding. He walked her down the aisle and then passed her on—sometimes unwillingly—to another male with whom he had made a contract. The whole ceremony of the father handing over the bride is rife with sexism. It is surprising this vestige of inequality has survived in the culture.

67. *Will the priest allow everyone with objections to the wedding to "speak now or forever hold your peace?"*

No, that is not part of the Catholic marriage rite either. That happens in movies and television.

In reality, though, the motive behind the question is still alive. The church is expected to find out if the partners are eligible for marriage (*Code of Canon Law* 1067). That is why the parish offers you sessions during your engagement and completes paperwork prior to the wedding. It is all part of the church's responsibility to make sure you are both free to marry and are entering this relationship with the right intentions.

It is a little late to ask if anyone has objections after people have walked down the aisle. We don't do that.

68. May "Here Comes the Bride" play when we walk down the aisle?

You may not assume the answer is yes. Many parishes do not allow this music for the wedding procession.

The traditional wedding march first appeared in Wagner's opera *Lohengrin*. It is played in Elsa's bridal chamber, not during the wedding procession. It gained popularity after it was used outside the opera for a royal wedding. But its secular origin keeps it off the list of preferred music in many parishes.

You may have noticed in the quotation from the *Rite of Marriage* above, that after describing the procession it says, "Meanwhile, the entrance song is sung." The preference in the liturgy is that the assembly of the faithful gathered for your wedding will sing a song of praise to God *during the procession* to set the tone for what will follow. The wedding is not about the coming of the bride. It is about the coming of the Holy Spirit, the gathering of the faithful, and the mystery of God's love.

Many couples enter to another piece of instrumental music, and then have everyone sing a song of praise when all have taken their places.

69. *My father has died and my mother has remarried. Who walks me down the aisle?*

It is up to you. The *Rite of Marriage* says that parents (in the plural) may escort the bride and groom. You may walk down with your mother and her husband. You may walk down with your mother. You may walk down with your groom. Or you may walk by yourself.

The point of your entrance is not to have an escort for your wedding. It is for you to enter as a minister of this celebration, a minister who will give your consent to a spouse.

70. Can my father and stepfather walk me down the aisle?

Again, the *Rite of Marriage* says of the procession, the bride and groom "may be escorted by at least their parents and the two witnesses." It does not further define who a parent is. A lot of this depends on your relationships in your family. The church places no additional demands on what may be a social matter.

Yes, both fathers could walk with you. Your mother could also. The groom's parents may also walk with him.

71. Should everyone stand when the bride starts down the aisle?

Actually, people should stand as soon as the procession begins—when the *servers* walk down the aisle. That is when they stand for a Sunday Mass, and your wedding should call for the same posture.

For some reason, people are in the habit of standing for the bride's entrance. But we are gathered as one body to give praise to God together, not to salute the bride.

You can help matters by suggesting that your song leader gesture for everyone to rise as soon as the entrance music begins and the procession starts into the church.

72. May we light a candle in memory of a deceased parent?

Yes, you should be able to do this. There is no specific provision for it in the *Rite of Marriage*, but this request should meet a courteous reply from your parish staff.

Be open to negotiating the placement of the candle. For example, it should not end up on the altar table itself. Nor should it be placed where it cannot be seen or where it obstructs people's view of the ceremony.

You may want to include a note in your printed program about the candle, so people will understand its significance. You might also place a picture of your parent next to the candle. But discuss this with the parish staff and see what advice you receive.

---

73. *Will we have to kneel? My fiancé isn't a Catholic and feels awkward about this.*

Your fiancé should not have to do anything she or he feels uncomfortable doing.

You should strongly consider the marriage ceremony without a Mass, which never calls for kneeling. All will stand or be seated.

If the wedding includes a Mass, there will be occasions when the assembly kneels. However, you could ask the presider if it would be acceptable for the two of you to stand during those times. The only time kneeling is expected during the Mass in the United States is from the Holy, Holy until the Great Amen. Even then, standing is acceptable for a "good reason" (Sacramentary, *General Instruction of the Roman Missal* 21).

The wedding kneeler is an archaic but persistent piece of furniture. It is usually placed in the sanctuary where the bride and groom have their backs to the assembly. It ordinarily comes without chairs, so that when the assembly and the presider are seated, the couple is kneeling. It is rather strange. Prior to the Second Vatican Council, the priest said Mass with his back to the people. Since then we have turned the priest around, but we still have not turned the couple around. The couple should be able to assume the same postures as the rest of the assembly, and it would help everyone's participation if the bride and groom were arranged so that all could see their faces.

If the bridal gown makes sitting impossible, the bride may not be suitably attired for worship.

74. *My partner is agnostic and doesn't want to say anything insincere during the ceremony. Will that be a problem?*

It should not be a problem. Your fiancé should say only those things that are honest and sincere.

The points might be minor. For example, your partner may not want to sing hymns or recite prayers, but would not object if others did so at the wedding. There should be no problem with that.

Other points may be more serious. Your fiancé may have objections to taking part in a Catholic celebration. In this case, you may obtain a dispensation from canonical form and have the wedding in a completely different context (*Code of Canon Law* 1127/2). Your parish priest should be able to arrange this.

75. *May we use the King James Version of the Bible for the readings?*

Catholics do not use the King James Version of the Bible for worship. We have a translation of the Scriptures approved for use in our lectionary, or book of readings.

We respect the Christian churches that use the King James Version, but in our opinion that translation, while beautiful, is defective because it does not reflect advances in biblical scholarship and is therefore not suited for our public worship.

76. Will people see and hear us when we give our consent?

Discuss this with your parish staff. Many presiders see to it that everyone can see and hear you, but others do not.

Regarding placement, it usually helps if the presider who asks and receives your consent stands between you and the assembly at that point of the service, facing the same direction as the people. That way, when you turn to face your minister, you face the people as well. You look at your partner while you give your consent.

Regarding hearing, ask about sound reinforcement. The people will want to hear you. Stand beneath a hanging microphone, move a floor mike close to you, station a server nearby with a mike, or have the groom wear a wireless mike. The thought of amplifying your voice may frighten you at first, but it will let your words of love resound throughout the church and the world.

If anyone in attendance has a hearing impairment, use an interpreter. The legally blind appreciate having speakers identify themselves.

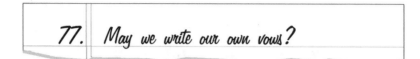

77. May we write our own vows?

The church gives you several options and asks you to choose one. Most people say, "I, N., take you, N., to be my (wife/husband). I promise to be true to you in good times and in bad, in sickness and in health. I will love you and honor you all the days of my life."

But others will say, "I, N., take you, N., for my lawful (wife/husband), to have and to hold, from this day forward, for better, for worse, for richer, for poorer, in sickness and in health, until death do us part."

Or the presider can ask you, "N., do you take N." and so on, using either formula, and you answer, "I do" (*Rite of Marriage* 25).

If you have nicknames as well as formal names, agree ahead of time which name you want to use at this point. Some couples think the solemnity of the occasion calls for the use of one's formal name. Others prefer to call the other by the names they commonly use. It's your choice.

By the way, we call this "the consent," not "the vows." It is the heart of the wedding. It is better not to tinker with the words. You want to make sure everyone understands that your consent is official.

78. *Do the vows have to include "love, honor, obey"?*

No. As you can see in the previous answer, we don't use that particular form of consent. And no partner says anything the other partner does not say. You are promising "to be true" to your partner, and your partner promises the same to you.

79. May we memorize the words of our consent?

O h, yes, and please do. This makes an outstanding spiritual preparation during the months before your wedding. Memorize those
words. Say them every day, several times a day. Make them a part of
you.

While you're at it, memorize this line, too: "N., take this ring as a
sign of my love and fidelity. In the name of the Father, and of the Son,
and of the Holy Spirit" (*Rite of Marriage* 28). These words, together
with your consent—these are your big lines.

In most weddings, the bride and groom repeat their consent phrase
by phrase after the presider, but the liturgy actually never envisions
this possibility. If memorization is a problem, you could read the lines
out of the book during the service. Just have one of the servers hold the
book for you as they do for the presider.

80. May we incorporate our Hispanic traditions in the wedding?

Yes, you may. But discuss this with your presider. There are many customs worth considering.

Godparents usually maintain a strong relationship with young people after the baptism and will have roles to play in supporting and celebrating the wedding. They may set the rings out for the bride and groom during the procession. They often help pay for the reception.

In another Hispanic tradition, the groom places twelve or thirteen coins, the *arras*, into the cupped hands of the bride. Originally, this symbolized his pledge to attend her fiscal needs. Today, many couples have a joint income, as well as the desire to share their goods with the needy. If the custom is retained, it may be reworded to reflect the contemporary situation more authentically.

Some couples ask for the *lazo*. This enormous double rosary may be placed around the couple for the nuptial blessing, for example, as a sign of their spiritual union.

81. Is the African tradition of jumping the broom permitted at a Catholic wedding?

There are couples who do it, but think this one through.

On the one hand, it comes from an African tradition and some couples see it as part of their ethnic heritage. On the other hand, the custom evolved in this country as a consequence of slavery.

Some African slaves came to the United States from tribes who ritualized marriage in this way. The bride and groom would literally jump over a broom, and that sealed their matrimonial consent. Slaves lacked the legal status for public marriage rites by a minister and often "jumped the broom" to get married in the United States.

The expression is still heard colloquially. "My friends jumped the broom," means they got married. The practice differed from Hispanic customs that augment the exchange of consent. Jumping the broom accomplished the consent.

Before you decide to add jumping the broom to your Catholic wedding, remember it might be interpreted as a symbol of slavery, not of freedom, and that it must not compete with the exchange of consent given orally by the couple. You are not married when you jump a broom. You are married when you give your consent.

82. Do we have to have rings?

Yes, the rings are important. There may be regions of the world where the exchange of rings would not fit in with the practice of the people. In those situations, bishops of those areas may produce a version of the rite that omits the rings or substitutes something else for them (*Rite of Marriage* 15). In the United States, however, we use two rings.

If there were some case of necessity (*Code of Canon Law* 1119), all that needs to happen for marriage is the exchange of consent before witnesses. But rings are a normal part of the ceremony.

83. When do we kiss?

Incredible as this sounds, there is no kiss in the Catholic marriage rite. You can tell it was written by celibate males.

In the version of the rite that includes Mass, it says, "At the words 'Let us offer each other the sign of peace,' the married couple and all present show their peace and love for one another in an appropriate way" (*Rite of Marriage* 35). A kiss would be very appropriate as part of the marriage ceremony itself.

The most logical place for the couple to kiss is after the exchange of rings. It signals the union of the couple in a spirit of joy.

84. May we use a unity candle?

Many couples exercise this option. Before the ceremony begins, parents or representatives from each family light a candle. Later in the ceremony, the newlyweds each light a third candle from the two their families have lit. This action occurs nowhere in the Catholic marriage rite, but it is being used widely.

Some parishes do not allow the unity candle. Its history is very recent compared with the other parts of the ceremony. It seems a duplication of what the consent and rings are expressing. If the other parts of the ceremony are done well, there may be no need for an additional visual symbol.

Also, the sharing of candlelight in the liturgy usually connotes the Easter Vigil or the rite of baptism. In both instances, light is drawn from the Easter candle to signify spreading the light of Christ. Usually we light multiple candles from one, not one from two.

Furthermore, many couples extinguish the candles lit by their families after they light the third one, the unity candle. It looks like they are extinguishing those relationships.

Nonetheless, the recurrence of the unity candle at weddings is amazingly strong. Couples apparently like its simple message of unity.

The candle, if used, should not be placed on the altar. The altar is for the Eucharist. Set up a separate table, visible to the assembly, but not obstructing their view.

If you want a unity candle, ask at your parish if that is all right. The best time to light it is probably after the exchange of rings. If you have no particular interest in the candle, you can leave it out. The rest of the ceremony will thoroughly express your love, honor your family, and symbolize your unity.

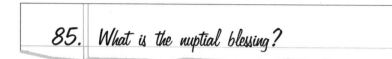

85. What is the nuptial blessing?

The priest or deacon who presides for your wedding gives you this special blessing for the occasion. Your marriage actually takes place when you give your consent to each other. The nuptial blessing is a prayer that God will grant you favor.

When marriage takes place at Mass, the blessing comes after the Lord's Prayer. Its placement there shows the parallel between the marriage covenant and the covenant of the Eucharist. God becomes one with us in the Eucharist, and the couple become one in their love and consent.

When marriage takes place outside of Mass, the nuptial blessing concludes the prayer of the faithful. The Lord's Prayer follows. A priest or deacon may give this blessing.

86. Why is the bride supposed to bring flowers to the statue of Mary?

The bride does not have to do this. It is completely optional. In fact, it does not appear in the Catholic marriage rite, although it is often included because of tradition.

Traditionally, near the end of the ceremony, the bride brought flowers to a statue of Mary in the church while the groom waited behind. This devotional exercise allowed her to pray for Mary's protection in her new marriage.

In today's efforts to equalize the sexes, and in the middle of a celebration of unity, it seems odd for the bride to go alone. Some couples go together to fulfill this tradition.

In the context of public worship, however, this private prayer does not fit well in the midst of the community's gathering. It would be like having everyone wait at Sunday Mass while one worshiper got up, walked to a statue, said a prayer, and then returned to the seat. Members of the assembly witness the giving of consent, but they participate in the common prayer of the wedding.

Still, the tradition remains popular with some Catholics because—well, because it is a tradition.

---

87. *May we have communion under both forms at the wedding Mass?*

Yes, and please do. The church encourages the faithful to share communion under both the forms of bread and wine (*General Instruction of the Roman Missal* 240). It represents a fuller sharing in the Eucharist.

It is inhospitable to remove this option from Catholics in the assembly.

Those who suffer celiac disease cannot consume any wheat product, and their only option for sharing communion may be from the cup. Have both forms available.

88. May communion ever be shared with those who aren't Catholics at a Catholic wedding?

Ordinarily, no, communion at a Catholic Mass is to be shared by Catholics only. The church's legislation is based on "the incomplete character of this communion [among Christians] because of differences of faith and understanding which are incompatible with an unrestricted mutual sharing of spiritual endowments" (*Directory for the Application on Principals and Norms on Ecumenism* 104c2). The Catholic Church is open to sharing Eucharist with Eastern Orthodox churches, but recognizes that they "may have more restrictive disciplines in this matter, which others should respect" (122). We do not offer communion to those of other churches and ecclesial communities because "eucharistic communion is inseparably linked to full ecclesial communion and its visible expression" (129).

An exception may be made in danger of death, or when the local bishop judges that the following criteria are fulfilled: "that the person be unable to have recourse for the sacrament desired to a minister of his or her own church or ecclesial community, ask for the sacrament of his or her own initiative, manifest Catholic faith in this sacrament and be properly disposed" (130–131). The pastor can only grant permission when the one requesting the Eucharist is in danger of death. The bishop otherwise makes the judgment.

Being present at a wedding, however, does not of itself fulfill the criteria. The church is aware of the special circumstances surrounding the marriage of two baptized Christians and admits that this "particular situation" should be considered when weighing the decision (159). However, "eucharistic sharing can only be exceptional and in each case the norms stated above concerning the admission of a non-Catholic Christian to eucharistic communion ... must be observed" (160).

It is for these reasons that marriage between a Catholic and someone of another religion may more suitably be celebrated without a Mass. Catholics who wish to share communion on the wedding day may participate at Mass at some other time of day before the wedding.

89. What if people who aren't Catholic go up to receive communion anyway?

They run the risk of being refused communion. Many communion ministers can tell by the way someone stands in line that he or she has never done this before. Some ministers decline communion to those who are not Catholics.

Some who are not Catholics, unaware of the discipline of our church, have presented themselves for communion and received it. We share the Eucharist on the honesty system and expect people to be informed and to respect our church's beliefs.

You could print a notice in your program about eligibility for communion. National Conference of Catholic Bishops copyrighted its "Guidelines for the Reception of Communion" in 1996 (see bibliography).

90. *If we had the wedding at another church,
everyone could go to communion,
but the Catholic Church would not recognize
the marriage, right?*

S low down. You can get permission for the wedding to take place in another church if one of you is not a Catholic. With a dispensation from canonical form, arranged by your Catholic pastor, the wedding that takes place in the other church will count for the Catholic Church as well.

But communion is another matter. Catholics are not supposed to share communion offered in another church, for the same reasons that we do not invite those of other faiths to share ours (*Directory for the Application on Principals and Norms on Ecumenism* 132). You still end up with the same problem: This great celebration of marital unity will not be a celebration of eucharistic unity.

> ### 91. Could a Protestant minister come to a Catholic wedding and offer communion to those who are not Catholics?

No, we are not supposed to do this one either. Think about how terribly divisive that would be to have separate communions at the same service.

When a Catholic marries another Christian in a Catholic church during a wedding outside of Mass, it is permissible to distribute communion from the tabernacle to the Catholics. When a Catholic marries an unbaptized person in a wedding outside of Mass, there is no provision for distributing communion. Whether or not there is Mass, only Catholics would be able to share communion. And communion outside of Mass is always an inferior solution to communion at Mass.

Again, when only one partner is Catholic, our usual recommendation is to have the marriage apart from Mass and communion. When there is no communion rite, the Scriptures become a focus for the ceremony. That puts everyone in the assembly on the same footing, and all can enter the prayer of the wedding more strongly together.

92. Can't a priest just invite everyone to communion? I know it has been done before.

Priests have done this, but the ecumenical directory does not give them the authority to do so. If you ask your priest to invite everyone to communion, you are asking him to do something the church does not allow.

93. May people throw rice after the ceremony?

A rice-throwing policy comes from the parish, so you will have to ask there. Rice is not part of the Catholic marriage rite.

Many churches expressly forbid throwing rice. Rice can be slippery and dangerous to guests. They may slip and fall. You could face legal problems if someone breaks a hip.

Other people throw birdseed, blow bubbles, or light sparklers in an attempt to give the ceremony a festive finish.

Ideally, people will be participating in song and spoken responses throughout the wedding and they won't need something at the end to make them feel suddenly involved in the celebration.

94. How much money are we supposed to give the priest and the church for a wedding?

Some parishes will assign a fee and they can tell you exactly what a wedding will cost. Others let you make a gift of your own choosing.

A typical church will incur many expenses in the preparation and celebration of your wedding. Staff members have been trained, buildings have been constructed, maintenance is continuous. A sizable gift from you will be greatly appreciated. Bigger than the one you are thinking about.

What means most to a parish, though, is a habit of giving regularly. The Catholic Church generally encourages its members to contribute 10 percent of their earnings to charities. But giving among Catholics is embarrassingly lower than it is among other denominations. Go ahead and figure out 10 percent of your income and see how close you are to the ideal. If you make giving to the parish a regular habit, you will help the community that is helping you. And if you can make a special gift to the parish at the time of your wedding, they will be very grateful.

95. Does the bride have to change her name after a Catholic wedding?

We have no rule about this. Changing the name is purely a matter of custom. Many women happily accept the new name. Others keep their old ones. Some hyphenate the names of the spouses.

What matters more is what is in the heart. The unity of the couple and their family will require more work than a change in name.

96. Am I excommunicated if I get married outside the Catholic Church?

No, "excommunication" is a formal term for a penalty that excludes someone from the sacraments and from leadership roles in the church's public life (*Code of Canon Law* 1331). It is brought about by a narrow range of specific offenses, ranging from a physical attack on the pope to having an abortion. Marriage outside the church does not cause the formal penalty of excommunication, but it does make you ineligible for the sacraments.

97. If I'm married outside the Catholic Church, may I still go to communion?

No, if you are married outside the Catholic Church, the church asks you to abstain from sharing the sacrament of communion with other Catholics. It is not a formal excommunication. You can still be active in a parish community, volunteer, and socialize. But you will not be eligible for communion.

Notice that divorce does not exclude someone from receiving communion in the Catholic Church. Divorced people may and do share in communion all the time. Marriage outside the church is what incurs the penalty.

98. *I love my partner and we just want to have a beautiful ceremony. It feels like the church doesn't care about us. If I get married somewhere else, does the church consider it a sin?*

The church does indeed care for you and wants you to have a beautiful ceremony. If you have trouble working out the details with your parish, keep trying, and remember the big picture. The details may not be as important as maintaining a good relationship with the church, especially as you are beginning this new life.

If you choose to be married somewhere else, your action is serious. You ask if it is a sin. You will know it is a sin if you do it knowingly and willfully, with the intent to do something wrong.

But try not to let it go that far. Keep trying to work things out.

99. *If I get married outside the Catholic Church, may I still have my children baptized Catholic and may they attend Catholic schools?*

Probably. Marriage outside the church does not of itself exclude you from having children baptized or enrolling them in Catholic schools. It may exclude you from serving as a godparent for someone else's children.

If you love the church enough to share the faith with your children through baptism and education, you will want to keep your marriage regularized with the Church as well.

100. *If I get married outside the church, how soon could I have the church recognize my*

Opinions differ, but many church leaders recommend about a year. Ask at your parish. They will know.

101. So tell me, why should I have a Catholic wedding?

A Catholic wedding is a celebration of faith that sets a couple on the road to mission in the church and community. It takes place in the context of a worship service in a sacred place. It brings together a community of believers who will pray for the couple and express their support. This community will also witness your consent, honor the seriousness of your commitment, and hold you to it.

A Catholic wedding will also give you the support of the entire church. Your wedding will take its place in a long line of ceremonies in which couples have consecrated their lives to each other and to God. It will happen in the embrace of a church that takes marriage seriously. A Catholic wedding will take place before a minister designated by the church for this service, to represent the whole community of the faithful.

A Catholic wedding will challenge you to live your faith in a new dimension. It will recognize the love that God has placed in your heart for your partner and it will challenge you to share that love with your children and with the community. On the strength of that love you will have greater ability for service. A Catholic wedding will remind you that your marriage is not just about you two. It is about a family. It is about the church. It is about community. It is about the world.

A Catholic wedding will give you a memory that will provide a source of strength for you as you face the struggles of life. You will know that your love is at your side and that Christ is inside your love.

A Catholic wedding will set your sights high. It will call you to live in faithfulness to God and to your spouse. It will call you to share the love and possessions you have with the needy.

A Catholic wedding will celebrate your love with the belief that God loved you first, and that God placed love within you. It will celebrate the presence of Christ in the church, and the presence of Christ in your marriage. A Catholic wedding will celebrate the mystery of love to its fullness.

That's why you should have a Catholic wedding. Congratulations, again! See you at church.

Bibliography

Documents

The Book of Blessings. Collegeville, Minn.: The Liturgical Press, 1989.

Catechism of the Catholic Church. 2nd ed. Vatican City: Libreria Editrice Vaticana, 1997. http://www.vatican.va/archive/catechism/ p2s2c3a7.htm

Catholic Household Blessings & Prayers. Washington, D.C.: National Conference of Catholic Bishops, 1988.

The Code of Canon Law: A Text and Commentary. Ed. James A. Coriden, Thomas J. Green, Donald E. Heintschel. Mahwah, N.J.: Paulist Press, 1985.

"Guidelines for the Reception of Communion." National Conference of Catholic Bishops, 3211 4th St., N.E., Washington, DC 20017-1194 (202) 541-3060. http://www.nccbuscc.org/liturgy/current/intercom.htm

International Committee on English in the Liturgy, Inc. *The Order of Mass.* Washington, D.C.: International Committee on English in the Liturgy, Inc., 1969.

International Committee on English in the Liturgy, Inc. *The Rite of Marriage.* Washington , D.C.: International Committee on English in the Liturgy, Inc., 1969.

Pontifical Council for Promoting Christian Unity. *Directory for the Application of Principles and Norms on Ecumenism.* Pontifical Council for Promoting Christian Unity, 1993. Http://www.vatican.va/roman_curia/ pontifical_councils/chrstuni/documents/rc_pc_chrstuni_ doc_25031993 _ principles-and-norms-on-ecumenism_en.html

Resources

About the Sacrament of Marriage. A Scriptographic Booklet. South Deerfield, Mass.: Channing L. Bete Co., Inc., 1982.

Champlin, Joseph M. *Together for Life.* Notre Dame: Ave Maria Press, 2000.

———. *Together for Life: Special Edition for Marriage Outside Mass.* Notre Dame: Ave Maria Press, 1998.

Coe, Victoria J. *Your Wedding Mass Planner.* Los Angeles: Franciscan Communications, 1989.

Covino, Paul, ed. *Celebrating Marriage: Preparing the Wedding Liturgy, a Workbook for Engaged Couples.* Portland: Pastoral Press, 1994.

Fleming, Austin. *Parish Weddings.* Chicago: Liturgy Training Publications, 1987.

Francis, Mark R., and Arturo J. Pérez-Rodríguez. *Primero Dios: Hispanic Liturgical Resource.* Chicago: Liturgy Training Publications, 1997.

Freund, John, and JoAnn Heaney Hunter. *Mirror of God's Love: Sacramental Marriage and the Difference It Makes.* Collegeville, Minn.: The Liturgical Press, 1991.

Gallagher, Rosemary, and John Trenchard. *Your Wedding: A Guide to Getting Married in the Catholic Church.* Liguroi: Liguori Publications, 1995.

Giandurco, Joseph R., and John S. Bonnici. *Partners in Life and Love: A Preparation Handbook for the Celebration of Catholic Marriage.* New York: Alba House, 1996.

Kippley, John F. *Marriage Is for Keeps: Foundations for Christian Marriage.* Wedding Edition with Marriage Rite and Readings. Cincinnati: The Foundation for the Family, Inc., 1993.

Kunde-Anderson, Mary Beth, and David Anderson. *Handbook of Church Music for Weddings.* Chicago: Liturgy Training Publications, 1992.

Marcheschi, Graziano, and Nancy Seitz Marcheschi. *Scripture at Weddings: Choosing and Proclaiming the Word of God.* Chicago: Liturgy Training Publications, 1992.

McAnany, Kathleen, and Peter Schavitz. *The Two Shall Be One: Preparing Your Church Wedding, a Workbook for Engaged Couples.* Liguori: Liguori Publications, 1994.

Richstatter, Thomas. *Before You Say "I Do": Four Things to Remember When Planning Your Wedding Liturgy.* Cincinnati: St. Anthony Messenger Press, 1989.

Szews, George R. *We Will Celebrate a Church Wedding.* Collegeville, Minn.: The Liturgical Press, 1983.

Your Catholic Wedding. Chicago: Liturgy Training Publications, 2001. Videocassette.

Index